# JOE

JANICE FREEMAN

ISBN 978-1-967361-38-0 (Paperback)
ISBN 978-1-967361-39-7 (Ebook)

Inquiries and Book Orders should be addressed to:

Leavitt Peak Press
17901 Pioneer Blvd Ste L #298,
Artesia, California 90701
Phone #: 2092191548

# Contents

# Introduction

*In a* book that I recently wrote, titled "The Family Secret," was a minor character named Joe, who married one of the major characters named Carlee. Carlee was from a Southern family who had moved to the North, long before she was born to her grandparent's eldest daughter, Clare. After moving North Carlee's grandfather was made the head of a very large pharmaceutical company and became the company's CEO.

Carlee's mother died when she was just a toddler, so she was raised by her grandparents. Carlee's father, Hugh was a medical doctor at the time of her mother's death. He had just completed the development of his Southern medical practice. Hugh thought it best to remain in the South and after he discussed this with Clare's parents, they all agreed it would be best for Carlee to be raised by them.

Hugh visited Carlee whenever he could and after several years went by, he informed his in-laws he had met someone he planned to marry. When Hugh's in-laws met his fiancée Dorothy, they were amazed at how much she looked like their deceased daughter Clare. Due to Hugh and Dorothy's impending marriage which would uproot Carlee, after much discussion with his in-laws it was decided that her grandparents would continue to raise her. However, her father and stepmother would visit back and forth which went on for years until two more children named Michael and June were born to them.

Carlee was a gem of a girl and lived with her grandparents all the way through high school. Her grandparents did not know how they were going to get along without her now that her college years were approaching. When it was time for her to go to college, Carlee decided to attend the same Southern college her mother and grandmother attended because of its excellent science program. Carlee did not fully realize, until she arrived at the school, the terrible racial prejudice which existed in the South. This was being addressed by the Civil Rights Movement under Dr. Martin Luther King Jr. as well as other Civil Rights Leaders.

Since Carlee lived all of her life in the North with her grandparents, she was influence by the Northern educational system, throughout her school years. This included attending some of the finest private schools because her grandparents were very wealthy. It also made it possible for Carlee to live harmoniously with all races and cultures, even though some of her grandparent's Southern beliefs remained in their home, but not outside of it. Their beliefs were handed down to Carlee in stories about the old South's history, leaving out the deep racial prejudice that still existed there. They both were from

Southern families whose ancestors going back three generations were from some of the richest families in the South. Carlee grew up with friends from other cultures including African Americans. Throughout her years at college, she did not allow the college's racist ideologies to influence who she was. When Carlee reached her junior year at college, she met Joe West, who would become her future husband. He was a Southerner who held to all the known racist beliefs of that period, having been raised on them since he was a small child. When Joe found out that Carlee was a Northerner and did not believe in racist behavior, he did everything he could to cover himself, because he truly fell in love with her and did not want to lose her. Joe surely would have lost Carlee, if she had known that his family had such racist beliefs, that went as far back to the beginning days of the Ku Klux Klan. At this time in their lives, Joe, and his father Dan, were very sympathetic to the Klan's ideology. Some of Dan's family members were still very active in the Klan's activities.

Though Joe and Dan were sympathetic and still held these beliefs toward the Klan, they did not participate in the Klan's activities. Through the years, Dan became a wealthy businessman and Joe was following his father in the business. If Dan was still actively participating in the Klan and it became known, it may have alienated some of their very good customers. The affection between Carlee and Joe grew into a wonderful love affair and as it developed, he was very careful not to ever let her see the racist side of him. When Carlee graduated from college, she and Joe married and were very happy together. After two years of marriage, Carlee gave birth to a beautiful 8-pound baby girl who they named Clare after Carlee's mother. Clare had blond hair and blue eyes just like her father Joe. Carlee, Joe, and other family members thought Clare was very beautiful. Everyone who saw the baby Clare at the hospital also spoke about how beautiful she was. Then, several days after Clare's birth, Joe had a life-changing experience outside the hospital nursery. The incident, though it was not an immoral one, made Joe want to end his and Carlee's marriage, even though he did not blame her for his decision. Where Joe was standing outside of the nursery, he could not be seen by anyone, however, he overheard a nurse mention to another nurse that the beautiful blonde baby in the nursery had African American blood. The nurse said she knew this because of the small marking on the lower part of her back which could have been thought of as a birthmark. The nurse also mentioned that no one would have ever suspected the baby's ethnicity by looking at her.

As soon as Carlee came home from the hospital, she noticed that something was wrong with Joe and it took several days before he let her know what was bothering him. What Carlee did not realize was that Joe had such a racist background making it impossible for him to ignore what he had found out. Joe wanted to divorce Carlee even though he realized that it was not her fault. Even though Eugene and

Joe had been best friends since they were children, Eugene never realized Joe would divorce Carlee over what had been revealed to him or he would have pleaded with Joe to stay with her because she was such an exceptional woman. The fact was, if Eugene had met Carlee first, he would have never let her go for any reason. Eugene's background had been full of racism like Joe's, but medical school had taught him the truth about the human body.

Joe explained to Carlee that he would take full financial responsibility for her and the child. Joe also made Carlee promise she would never reveal his reason for divorcing her to her grandparents and he would never reveal the reason to his parents. Carlee always thought Joe would come to himself because of the loving relationship they had, but he never did. So, she moved back to her grandparent's home, never telling them the reason for the divorce. Carlee's grandparents were so happy to have her back home, they almost did not care what the reason was besides they absolutely loved the baby. However, Carlee's divorce and move back home, left her in a state of depression. Her grandparents were determined they would do anything to help Carlee get well. In time they did and Carlee had a much better outlook on life and the situation had a very good ending. It took a while but with their wonderful loving care and not sparing any expense to get her back in school things turned out better than they could have ever imagined.

# 1

## Joe's Father Dan

Imagine a young boy in the deep South being raised on a thirty-acre farm, living in a run-down house, with five other siblings, in deep poverty. His father and mother are not well educated and are looked down upon by their neighbors because they are so poor and also illiterate. Neighbors who were also farmers, as well as plantation owners sent hand-me-down clothing from their children to the family and what they could wear, size wise would be distributed among them. They were barefoot when they walked to school which was seasonal because the children had to help their father work their farm. There were seasons when they did not have as much to do in helping their father run their farm so they played games with their older brother, Dan. Dan later became the father of Joe, who this story is all about. As mentioned, Dan who was the oldest child in the family was taught a lot of things by his father, which Dan taught to his younger sisters and brothers. Even though they were poor, they were a loving family.

Usually on Sundays and other special occasions, they wore the shoes that came from the hand-me-down packages, which were pretty worn. Because the shoes were worn, cardboard had to be placed on the sole. The clothing they received kept them covered even though they were not always the child's perfect size.

Dan was a lanky young man, who greatly helped his father on their farm and looked out for his younger brothers and sisters. He helped them with their lessons and to learn their chores and did not mind being responsible for them. The children looked up to Dan because even though he wasn't well educated, he seemed to know a lot and this made them feel secure around him. Because he was the older child he always looked out for his brothers and sisters and helped his parents with them. The story that Dan's father used to tell the children was when he was 18 years old, his best friend, TJ who was 19 received a call from his Uncle Joseph, who had moved to the North and was working in a factory. He told his nephew he could get him a good union job in the North. He also told TJ if he left the South and come North, he could help him get established. TJ made the decision to go, knowing this was a great opportunity. The house that TJ was living in was left to him by his grandfather and though it was structurally sound, cosmetically within and without it had been very badly neglected. The good thing was that it stood on 30 acres of good farmland. Knowing he would be going for good except for occasional visits back and forth, TJ sold Dan's father the property for $1.00. He knew Dan's father wanted to get married and this would allow Dan's father in-law to accept him as their daughter's husband because he had a home to bring her to. Dan's father's future wife was 16 years old when all this happened. This was the home that Dan and his brothers and sisters grew up in. TJ came back and forth to visit staying with Dan's father, but as the years went on the visits grew more infrequent. While living in the North, TJ married and had children but because of the run-down condition of Dan's father's house, his wife didn't want to come to visit anymore feeling she was above Dan's father's family economically. TJ stayed in the North for the rest of his life and after the first five years of visiting the South, TJ and Dan's father didn't see each other anymore and only sent cards at Christmas. Dan's father was always very grateful to TJ for making a way for him to get married and have a home and property.

One year Dan's father got seriously ill, so Dan and his brothers and sisters had to run the farm up until harvest time. Because the farm was so small, Dan's father also had to hire Dan out to a plantation owner whose land was attached to their land. Dan was able to work his farm, with his siblings help, as well as working the plantation owner's land. The income Dan brought in literally saved his family that year. While working on this plantation, Dan observed the latest methods that were used for raising crops and he also became acquainted with the newest type of farm equipment. With this knowledge, he knew that he could properly plant the crops and to also learn how to care for the livestock.

As he worked, he dreamed about how one day he would have a large farm of his own and be able to have similar equipment. Dan loved farming and he knew within his heart this was what he wanted to do for a living when he grew up, so anything he could learn about farming his ears and eyes were sharp and always wide open to it.

The plantation owner, knowing the family's situation, sent Dan home with extra vegetables and fruits to help them out. Dan worked extra hard for him because of this and showed in many ways his appreciation. This made the plantation owner have a real respect and fondness for Dan even though he believed that he would never reach the level of the wealthy plantation owners around Dan, including himself. However, he still admired Dan because he tried so hard to learn better methods that he could incorporate in the work he did on his father's small farm.

Because some of Dans' father's land touched this man's plantation, the plantation owner gave Dan's father extra acreage, bringing the size of his farm up to 60 acres, which helped out quite a bit and brought in more income.

Also, in one of the clothing packages that was given to the family, there was a lot of clothing that was new and it just so happened that they fit Dan very comfortably and was he happy. His mother told him that the really new clothing had to be worn on

Sunday for church and especially the shoes which were like brand new. That Sunday when Dan went to church, he was bathed and really dressed up and he felt so good imagining himself to be a young man of means owning a huge farm and growing all kinds of fruits and vegetables and having all the great equipment he needed to run a farm. Dan realized it was a dream, but he held on to it very tightly and continued his life on the farm doing his best.

Of course, by the next year, because he was growing so quickly, the clothes didn't fit him as they had and they now were becoming hand-me-downs to his brothers. Since his family was considered very low class, the only thing that made them feel better about themselves was the fact that they were members of the Ku Klux Klan and knew because of this they were superior to the African American community that was also working on these large plantations and farms. Some of these African Americans also owned their own farms and some of these farms were a good size. Dan and his family resented this and participated in harmful practices of the Klan by harassing these farmers. Dan's father, grandfather, and great grandfather told their children some horrendous tales about their treatment of the African Americans and some of it was very bad and of course some of it was exaggerated but those tales that were true were bad enough.

Dan had to work so hard that he didn't have time to get heavily involved in the Klan's activities. However, he did attend their meetings with his brothers and sisters when children were allowed to go. As Dan got taller and stronger, his father hired him out because he was such a smart worker and good at whatever he did. This allowed Dan to keep some of his own money. When Dan's father recovered from his illness, he was able to work his extra acreage. The children who had gotten older and were still living at home, were able to help him. Farming the extra acreage raised Dans' father's income for his family and things began to gradually get much better.

Because of Dan's skills, other plantation owners wanted him to come and work for them. They paid him well and he was finally made overseer on one of the larger plantations. His employer always gave Dan extra produce to take home at harvest time and Dan's father who hunted, taught him how to hunt to provide the meat that the family needed which was small game and sometimes larger animals.

As Dan acquired more finances, he bought more farmland and the amount of this land grew larger and larger. His reputation for producing excellent products was appreciated by the Whites and the African Americans who did not have large farms and worked in other occupations. A lot of these were mostly Dan's and later his son Joe's customers.

After Joe grew up, there were also smaller retail businesses growing up around them wanting to increase their business and they began to try to draw Joe's father's customers by accommodating them, especially his African American customers. They were somewhat successful, but Dan was an excellent businessman and saw the need to cover his racist behavior to keep those customers. Joe also was pulling away from his father's behavior because he was learning that money spent is not racist. It took a while, but the change in his business dealings seemed to have brought about a very lucrative return for both of them, so Joe kept going on encouraged by his father to always do his best especially, in his business dealings.

In the past some of these men that Dan worked for showed him how to do things in a better way than he was used to doing them and when they showed Dan it didn't matter what race or who they were, he would always listen to them in order to learn the best way to farm. Dan did give them credit for showing him what he had learned from them and always treated them with great respect as long as what they were showing him was serving his purpose. Dan also would thank them even though he still held on to his old racist ideas. Because of the Civil Rights movement, Dan also realized that he no longer could be as open about his racist attitude as he had been in the past because he didn't want anything to interfere with his business which always came first. Because of Dan's many insecurities growing up, he didn't correct his son Joe's negative behavior toward African Americans and let him grow up with very racist attitudes toward those African Americans who worked for Dan on his farm and others in the general population. By this time, Dan's farm could be considered very large and operating well. He was determined to succeed in life and to bring his only son along with him. So, he taught Joe everything he knew and raised and encouraged him to always work in an excellent way, having him work alongside his exceptional workers and to learn from these workers how to do the job well. These workers, Dan did not allow Joe to disrespect. All of Dan's workers knew what he believed about them in his heart but they also knew if they did a fine job, they at least got his respect. Dan was a true opportunist knowing how far to go in situations that would help his business to grow and give him favor with the customers that he dealt with.

Dan had a mechanic in his employ who knew everything about cars and farm machinery. Joe really admired him so, Dan encouraged Joe to stay close to him because Joe loved cars and this man patiently taught him all about cars and farm machinery. Joe was raised with a lot of prejudice against African Americans, but there were some men working for his father that he encouraged Joe to listen to because like Dan, they were excellent farmers and knew how to get the job done. As Joe grew up on the farm his father always tried to express to him how important it was to give each job he worked on his best and if there was a better way to learn something, he encouraged Joe not to hold on to the old way of doing it but instead to learn the better way which would work in Joe's favor. Like his father, he was becoming an outstanding farmer and was being recognized as exceptional in the way he did his work. As time went on, Joe almost became as good as his father.

Dan met Joe's mother when he was young and he was very attracted to her. Her name was Maureen and not only was she very pretty, but she came from a family that was economically better off than Dan's family. During the time that they were courting Dan's family would have been considered "poor White trash." But everyone knew that Dan was exceptional in his family and was truly making something out of himself. Maureen was better educated and had wonderful training from her mother, in taking care of a home. Her father also provided well for the family as a farmer. They were racist like Dan's family, but not as extreme. Maureen's mother had trained her and her brothers and sisters to keep themselves neat and clean and to keep their home the same way. They also had very good manners. Joe's father Dan couldn't help but be attracted to her because marrying her would help him to move up in the world from his situation. Her family liked Dan because even though he was from a poor background he was very hardworking and ambitious, even as a very young man he was ready to put her in her first home. In those early years he also had already obtained enough land to start a very good-sized farm. He was very respectful to her parents and helped them whenever he could and they grew very fond of him. They also like the way he provided for their daughter Maureen after they got married. Sadly, after Dan and Maureen married, they lost two of their first children through miscarriages. Maureen was very broken up about it for several years. However, Dan was such a good provider that his wife began to try to emulate the wealthier people in the community and those that would be considered middle class. This kept her very busy and when she got pregnant with Joe, her husband was able to put her into a large, beautiful home with hired help who were all African American. The house had 14 rooms and a section for the household's hired help who wanted to live in.

# 2

## Joe's Early Life

When Joe was born, Maureen was absolutely thrilled and loved having, as she called him "that fine boy". Because she had help, she could keep up with her very busy lifestyle. To help her with baby Joe, she considered hiring a nanny who would also help with the housework. The woman that was recommended for this position was named Mattye who had a baby daughter named Ida. Mattye had worked on one of the larger plantations in the area taking care of the worker's children. She did this from childhood because working out in the fields in the hot sun, on the plantation made her ill. Even after Mattye became older she still had this problem with the heat. However, the plantation owner had heard how well she took care of her mother's younger children and also her parent's house. He got the idea that if he hired her to take care of the workers children in a house on his planation that he could hire more women full time including Mattye's mother and he could pay Mattye a good salary. Of course, her mother and father were pleased with this idea because it allowed her mother to work full time and Mattye would also make a good salary. What was unusual about Joe's mother Maureen, was she was trained to keep a spotless home by her mother. Her brother and sister also learned to keep their home in very good order. Maureen's mother always kept her children and her husband clean and very neatly dressed. Maureen's parents were educated to the eighth grade, but his mother Maureen finished high school and married Dan right after her graduation. This is mentioned because when Maureen got her own large house and could afford hired help, she knew how a house should be kept and was able to direct those helping her on how to take care of her home. Whenever anyone visited, it looked like it was not even lived in. Of course, Dan loved Maureen's qualities because it made him look good and also inspired him to keep the outside of their house in impeccable condition.

Their house was large and because of this there were always cousins living with them, so growing up Joe always had small children to play with. They came to stay with them at different periods of time and neither Dan nor Maureen seemed to mind them coming. These children were mostly from Dan's side of the family. Maureen's family was typically Southern, but they were not hardened racists like Dan's family. Therefore, within the house, Maureen did not allow Joe to show disrespect to the hired help who were working for her and Dan. Dan backed Maureen up in this in order to please her. Dan demanded this behavior within the household even from those members of his own family who lived there, although at their homes they had been used to this very bad behavior.

Maureen, who was trying to keep up with her wealthy neighbors, loved Joe but she spent very little time with him because of shopping sprees and a very busy social life. Though Maureen had friends, she never reached the place in society she longed for. However, she still tried to better her life even though the wealthier people near Maureen's neighborhood could see that she was not of upper society. Maureen dressed well, drove a beautiful car, lived in a beautiful house and she and Dan went on some very expensive vacations. She had a cook in the house and other servants who kept her house beautiful, but at that time her friends and acquaintances were not Southern gentry. In time Maureen and Dan became extremely wealthy, living as well as their richest neighbors. As the years went by, they became so prosperous, they began to look down on some of the neighbors. The neighbors started to become more accommodating to Dan and Maureen, as their business grew very large and they grew more prosperous.

Joe loved his mother because she was so pretty and she was affectionate with him but the several miscarriages left a hole in her heart, so she stayed busy doing the things that she liked to do with friends and acquaintances. She was very nice to the help that worked in the house and did kind things for all of them. Because the house was large enough, as mentioned, some of the help lived in a certain section of the house and some of them were there for many years. Dan loved Joe, but he knew when Joe started private school that he was not as polished as Joe's classmate's rich fathers and even Dan's grammar was a bit rough. With his wife's help, he tried to work very hard on his grammar because he had such a thriving business. Dan had been a racist since he was young and his family had been so for generations. His own father's people who were Klansmen had done some terrible things to the African American people in the past, but as the years went on a lot of this behavior was modified because of the Civil Rights Movement. As the South's treatment of African Americans started showing up in the Northern papers, the Southern communities did not seem to address these serious law issues. More White people in the country began to get involved and joined the marches under Dr. Martin Luther King Jr. Some of their lives were taken because of this, it got so bad it finally had to be addressed by the Federal Government, even though it took quite a while for them to get involved in the way that they should have. Army troops had to finally be sent into Southern towns to keep the occupants under control because their behavior had gotten so terrible especially when the African American students started attending the White schools. The White crowds surrounded these schools calling the little children terrible names and threatening them. When older African American students started attending the White colleges the crowds got even worse but by this time soldiers were lining up to protect these students as they attended their first day at these all-White colleges. It was a horrendous struggle, but as time went on things got more under control and gradually people's hearts began to change for the better. Even though up to today there are some die hard people still left in some of these areas who would like to see racial segregation being enforced.

# 3

# Mattye

This Chapter is about Mattye, the lady who Maureen hired with her daughter Ida who played such an important role in Joe's life. The qualities Mattye possessed had to be shown. There are so many gems in her character that have to be revealed and cannot be ignored. Mattye is introduced at the beginning of the story as Joe's nanny, however, she became like a second mother to him and Ida became like a sister to Joe. There was genuine love between the three of them. As mentioned, Mattye had been one of the workers on a large plantation near Maureen's house. She was fortunate because for years she had a paid position on the plantation where she worked taking care of the children of the employees and her reputation for childcare was well known. Mattye worked taking caring of children because, from a young age, she could not work out in the hot sun so the plantation owner gave her this job. This freed up many of his female workers to work in the fields full time. From a very young age, being the oldest girl in her family, Mattye had to stay home with her siblings and take care of them while her parents worked in the fields. The other parents let the owner know how well she took care of her siblings and her parent's house. Hearing this gave him the idea of letting her take care of all the young children of his workers at one of his extra houses on the plantation and he would give her a nice salary. Her parents were pleased because it freed her mother up to work for the owner on a full-time basis and also to collect most of what Mattye was being paid.

When Mattye grew older, she was paid a full-time salary by the plantation owner. When Mattye turned 17, she married one of the workers on the plantation and finally received all of her pay. They were happily married for about two years before she got pregnant. Mattye's husband convinced her that it would be good for him to go North to find a better paying job and he would send for her as soon as he found one. When he first left, he wrote to Mattye often, however, his letters became less and less as the months went on. She let him know when the baby was born but she still didn't hear from him. Soon his daughter was almost a year old and Mattye's husband still hadn't come back. She moved back with her parents, and she paid them weekly rent, and still took care of the plantation employee's children at the same place the owner had originally provided. She really believed her husband when he told her that one of the main reasons for him wanting to go North was not only to get a better job but that the baby due would grow up under better circumstances. Of course, she was delighted to hear that and really held on to the hope that he was coming back for the both of them. He still hadn't come back by the time the baby was born even though she let him know that they had a little girl. She finally faced the fact that he was not coming back and she would have to raise their daughter by herself and that he probably got involved with someone else up North. She had heard about situations like this. She was unhappy for a while but the baby was so cute and such a happy baby that Mattye concentrated on her and dreamed of the things she was going to do with her. She finally got over him and she didn't seem to want to date anybody else even though there were some men working on the plantation that were interested in her. She continued her job encouraged by the owner to stay on since she had pleased all the parents with her childcare. Her reputation had spread to the other plantations and Maureen, Joe's mother had heard about her and her baby daughter from one of her friends. Her friend put her in touch with Mattye. When she interviewed Mattye, Maureen explained to her that she needed someone to take care of her two-year-old son. When she explained to her what came with the job, Mattye became interested. It came with a substantial raise, her own room in Maureen's house which had a bathroom and a small patio outside of the back door of the room where she could sit in the evenings. She would also have Sundays off. Mattye liked having Sundays off because she could attend her church and this really made her happy. Maureen told Mattye that she already had a cook and that she and Ida could eat the food that she cooked for breakfast, lunch, and dinner. Mattye and Ida would also eat with the family. Maureen would plan the meals and would do the food shopping including any extra food that Mattye and her daughter would like her to pick up. Mattye was a very attractive African American woman with very good manners and was neatly dressed when interviewed which was one of the reasons that Maureen wanted to hire her. Ida was absolutely adorable with dimples and black curly hair. Maureen fell in love with Ida because she had no daughters having experienced two miscarriages one of which was a girl and those relatives now living in the house with her and Joe were boys. Mattye accepted the job and even Dan grew very fond of Ida. After hiring Mattye, Maureen gave Mattye and her daughter the lovely room that she promised with a White ornate twin bedroom set. There was also room for a crib, which Maureen purchased since Ida was only a year old and not able yet to sleep in her own twin bed. Mattye gave her notice to the owner of the plantation explaining to her boss all that Maureen offered her and Ida but she also let him know that she appreciated everything he had done for her through the years when taking care of the employee's children. Her employer knew Maureen and Dan and told Mattye that whatever Maureen promised her she would get, and more.

Maureen loved to decorate, so she filled Mattye's room with beautiful things that both of them could appreciate such as matching furniture, bedspreads and curtains, lamps, plants, and pictures. When Mattye saw all that Maureen was doing, she was so pleased that she made up her mind that day that she and Ida were going to stay with these people as long as she could. She had thought in the past of going North as her husband did, to better her life but now she felt that it was the right move for her to remain in the South at Maureen and Dan's home. Mattye was there many years and never once regretted her decision.

Because Mattye had so much experience with children, she potty- trained Joe almost immediately and Joe seemed to take to her right away, which pleased Maureen. Since Joe and Ida were so close in age, they played together, ate together, and took naps at the same time. Joe and Ida played in a very nice nursery full of toys for boys and girls provided by Maureen. From the very beginning, both children got along very well and Joe absolutely loved Ida and Mattye. As Ida grew, Maureen assigned her different little jobs caring for the house. Mattye received extra pay for these little jobs and of course she saved most of the money toward Ida's future education. Mattye loved Joe as if he were her own child and with both the children so close it made her job very pleasant.

Even though Joe was raised in a racist environment because of his father's influence, it didn't seem to affect him inside the home. As mentioned, his mother Maureen never allowed any kind of racist talk in the house although some of Joe's poorer cousins who came to live with them were used to this kind of talk in their homes. They were able to live with Dan and Maureen from time to time because the house had 14 rooms. These relatives were mostly Dan's relatives and Maureen and Dan were certainly very kind to them and wanted them to have a better life. Mattye watched over all the children and like Joe they seemed to love Mattye even though she was African American. They had all come out of homes where they were encouraged to disrespect African Americans but at Maureen's house, they knew this was not happening. Mattye definitely had wonderful mothering skills and because of this Maureen and Dan allowed her to discipline all the children in the house. She seemed to have some very effective methods disciplining children which she taught herself while caring for so many children at the house on the plantation. It also allowed Maureen to have more time to spend on her outside activities. Dan also knew that Maureen's family was far above his socially and this was what attracted him to her. However, her family still had the same racist ideas that Southern families practiced at this time but some Southern families were not as blatant in these behaviors as others and Maureen's family was one of them.

Mattye wanted the best for her daughter so she trained her very carefully as to what she was to do to fit in to this White environment that they were now living. She did not want Ida to grow up feeling inferior to the other children that lived in the house. So instead, Mattye always made Ida feel that she was an exceptional girl and that one day she would grow up to be an extraordinary woman. Without realizing it, Maureen helped this along because of her affection for the child and because she didn't allow any racist talk in the house. As mentioned, her husband backed her up in this because he really loved his wife even though he was a sold-out racist but he wanted to really please Maureen. She also was a very good wife to him and kept a beautiful house.

Because there were no other girls in the house, when school time came about for Ida, Maureen took her shopping for her school clothes every year at the best department stores in town, paying for everything. While Ida was in these different stores some of the White women who brought their own daughters to shop for school clothes resented seeing Ida with this White woman. When they complained to management, it was explained to them that she was not trying any clothes on and this appeased their anger. These women didn't realize that Maureen was such a good customer who spent thousands in this and others stores. The owner of the store had his employees figure out Ida's size so everything that Maureen bought her was a perfect fit. The store's staff was warned by their employer not to mistreat Maureen or Ida when they were shopping but to give them the best service. When school was over, Maureen took Ida shopping again for play clothes for the summer. To show the character of Maureen, she also shopped for Dan's nephews but not with the same care as she did with Ida. This was because Maureen liked pretty girl things and loved having a little girl to dress up.

It was a strange dilemma that on the inside of the house everyone who lived there seemed to get along as a great family, but once they stepped outside, their racist attitudes were revived but not toward Mattye and Ida.

Ida did her chores well and she was taught by her mother that keeping her things neat, pleased Maureen, who always wanted her house kept in good order. Sometimes Maureen would bring Ida a new doll or some great new toy that the girls Ida's age liked and were playing with at that time. Ida was always happy with Maureen's special surprises. Mattye not only watched out for the children in the house but, she also did extra jobs that were not expected of her which surprised Dan and Maureen. Mattye more or less ran the whole house in a loving way, making sure that all the hired help who worked there were well supervised. Like the children, the hired help cooperated with Mattye because they knew how much Dan and Maureen respected her opinions and advice and appreciated her work ethic. All the help in the household got along well and knew that Dan and Maureen had a special affection for Mattye, so they tried to work well with her. Dan even planned to have Ida driven to the segregated school she attended which was quite a distance from their house. Maureen thought the walking distance was too far for Ida. The driver, who was African American not only drove her to school but also went to pick her up after school each day and sometimes had to wait for her because of some after school activity. Most people attending Ida's school thought the driver was a relative had no idea about the beautiful house that Ida lived in. Mattye taught Ida not to brag about her wonderful life. With Joe's help she got through all her grades with very high marks and she was well thought of at school. Ida never thought that she was better than anyone else and she always shared with those friends at school that may have needed her assistance. Ida's kindness endeared her to her classmates. With Joe helping her with her schoolwork, Ida was able to help some of her classmates who were having difficulty with their assignments. She would even stay in the classroom with them missing play time at recess, but it didn't seem to bother Ida because her mother always taught her to be helpful. Because of Joe helping Ida with her schoolwork, Ida always did outstanding work and she received many awards. Mattye was grateful because she realized that she did not have the educational background that Ida needed. Because Joe was a year ahead of her in his private school and had already been taught these subjects in a masterful way that Ida was now learning. His school was the best private school in the whole area and only the wealthiest children in that area attended that school. So, Joe already knew about all the subjects that she was being taught since he was a year ahead of her.

As the years went on, Ida was able to get a four-year scholarship to a very good African American college and she graduated from there with a four-year degree in business with honors. Dan, Maureen, Joe and Mattye attended her graduation. Dan gave her a large sum of money as a graduation gift because Ida wanted to travel to the North. She was going North to interview at a junior interior decorating college where she had already applied and also to look for work in that field. Ida loved decorating and she did find a good job in that field as well as a school that taught all the subjects she needed to know for interior decorating for the wealthy.

Mattye stayed with the family until she was 60 years old then passed away because of heart failure. The family took her passing very hard and even the cousins that had lived in the house wept. Ida had done very well on her decorating jobs and got an excellent job in the North and continued school there for interior decorating, which she learned to love by watching Maureen. She came home for her mother's funeral and she was received very well and was invited to stay in her mother's room for as long as she needed to before going back North. Dan gave her some money to travel with and to also buy some things to remember her mother by which Ida did. Because of Maureen's decorating influence, Ida became a famous interior decorator specifically for the rich and famous. So as her mother predicted she did become a great woman and developed a wonderful business in interior decorating. Ida invited Maureen to her beautiful home in the North and Maureen was very impressed with how African American people lived in Ida's beautiful neighborhood. She attended church with Ida and loved the service especially the choir. Ida and Maureen wrote back and forth and sent holiday cards throughout the years until in her late 60's Maureen passed away. Ida did go back for Maureen's funeral and wept along with all those in the family. When she finally did return to her lovely home in the North, she took one of the African American young boys named Paul with her. Ida asked Dan and Paul's mother's permission to take him, promising that she would send him back each summer. Mattye and Maureen always mentioned how bright Paul was from a little boy, so Ida wanted him to have a chance to get a good education in one of the top private boy's schools in the North. Because Paul was so smart, he received scholarships all the way through school and Ida paid for anything extra. He was also excellent in sports and the student's parents who attended his games looked forward to seeing him play and invited him to their homes to have fun with their children. Because she never had children, she treated him like her own son. In thinking about why she never had children, brings to mind the fact that she never married even though she was a very attractive and prosperous woman. Also, she was very close to Joe almost to the point that thinking about it hard enough, she may have had more than sisterly affection for him. Because of racial injustice and where she lived while growing up, she couldn't allow herself to entertain more than a sisterly relationship to him. She could not reveal it to anyone in the home, including her mother. She was also close enough to Joe that she knew he would never entertain marrying outside of his race. Even though there were very fine gentlemen that tried to win her affection and many professional women would have been happy to marry them, she knew in her heart it would not have been fair to these men because of this great love she had for Joe. Sometimes she would question herself by saying "why can't you let these feelings go when you know that it is a hopeless situation". Though she questioned this many times, it was those strong feelings that would not subside. She knew in her heart, that she could never love another man the way she loved Joe. So, she tucked away those feelings as deep inside of her as they could go. However, she still had strong maternal feelings and wanted children so Paul became a blessing to her.

As a college graduate in business herself and having an associate degree in Interior decorating, she was able to support Paul through his school years very well because her associate degree in interior decorating and her bachelor's degree in business made this financially possible. As he grew into manhood, he decided to settle in the North and continued to live with Ida like her own son and he earned an Electrical Engineering Degree. Paul eventually married a very lovely well educated young lady with a Civil Engineering Degree.

He and his wife had two children and they were just like Ida's own grandchildren. Paul supported his biological mother in her old age. She was still living in the South, but Paul tried to get her to move North. Paul's mother would visit, but she just did not want to live in the North. Paul would take his family to see his mother during the summers. The children were always glad to see their grandmother and the rest of their family but were anxious to get back to their friends and get back to Ida whom they called Nana. Another reason Paul's mother wanted to stay in the South was because she had other children and grandchildren there. She would only stay about two weeks when visiting Paul in the North and then want to go back home. She continued to live in the South with her family and he continued to visit her until she passed away many years earlier than Ida. Since his children were grown, he seldom traveled back to the South unless it was for special occasions, such as weddings or graduations. In Ida's later years, Paul and his children took care of her until she passed away in her late 70's.

# 4

## Joe's High School Years

When Joe was very young, he played with some of the children of his father's hired hands and only when he was very angry with them, did he called them names or made fun of them. He got very close to some of them even into their teen years. However, when he first started private school at age 5, his friendships with White children developed and he picked up many of their racist behavior, which he thought was correct. Because the students that he was in school with thought their behavior was right, Joe was edged on until it became an integral part of his behavior that lasted all the way through high school. Because his mother and father did not encourage bad behavior in the home, it was like living in two separate countries. Outside the home Dan did not correct Joe's racism. However, he did correct it when he thought somehow it affected the business. He also corrected him if he saw that Joe was benefiting from someone teaching him a part of the business that he needed to learn. Even though Dan, Joe's father, had attained great wealth through pure hard work in his business dealings, in his heart he realized that he had come out of poverty. However, looking down on African Americans gave Dan a feeling of superiority. In his earlier years, Dan and his family were always viewed as low class by the Southern gentry in the community near where he lived. However, Dan was recognized by all of them as a man who had truly pulled himself up by his bootstraps and had a natural ability when it came to the land. Dan bought more and more land and this caused him to reach the place that he and his family were as rich as some of his neighbors who already possessed very great wealth in their community. Dan had never gone to college, but anything to do with the land no one could do it better and of course, he brought his son Joe along with him by teaching him everything he knew about horticulture. Dan demanded excellence from him and Joe pursued Dan's interests. Joe learned to do everything well because of his father's high expectations. When Joe was in his early years at high school, he still had to ride the school bus. He and his friends would get African American names out of the phone book at home and call them on the telephone. They knew the neighborhoods that these African American people lived in so they would make fun of them by calling them vulgar names or talk using their accents and insulting them and cursing them. When the people hung up, Joe and his friends would call back several times laughing as hard as they could. One person they called said "You know God doesn't like ugly so you must be a very ugly person". Getting a reply like that really surprised them and Joe never forgot it. Joe and his friends would also throw old dirty rags out of the school bus window at the African American students walking to school and made fun of how they looked, their shapes, and how they spoke. When coming home from school Joe and his friends threw lunch bags with garbage inside toward them as the buses were flying by taking the White student's home. Sometimes Joe who was the ringleader, and his friends threw Kool- Aid on the African Americans' clothing and laughed all the way home about it. They would also hit them with pieces of fruit shot from a sling. At one time, it got so bad that the police had to follow the school bus because so much garbage was being thrown on the street in front of White people's houses. These people knew it wasn't the African American students who were at fault. The police presence helped curb this activity, but the White students were not disciplined for their bad behavior even though some of them came from the richest families in town and they attended a prominent private school.

Some of the crimes committed by the Ku Klux Klan were stories told by Dan to Joe when he was in his pre-teens. These stories included what Joe's father Dan experienced with his father, grandfather, and great-grandfather against the African American community. There were lynching, tar and feathering, dragging men chained to the back of moving trucks, and killing farm animals, which deprived African

American men of their livelihood. The Ku Klux Klan set some homes on fire, while people were inside sleeping, killing them all. The Klan broke into local jails taking prisoners out for lynching, decapitations, and emasculations in the woods. Sometimes women were harmed, but it was not the rule unless some of these Klansmen were drunk and wanted to harm them sexually.

The law hardly ever brought charges against the Klan unless it was so heinous that even some Klansmen felt it went too far. Later, when African American people tried to march to vote, those in line were mowed down by automobiles or shot. The Sheriff's men threatened their lives if they didn't disperse. The African American men were not always docile but retaliated in clever ways by killing their perpetrators. What was terrible about this was the law would charge whoever they picked up, whether they were guilty or not. It was not until the late 1950s into the 1960s when some people from the North got involved after seeing so much in newspapers and on television, how these African Americans were treated. This caused the Klan to begin to curtail a lot of its dirty work and these heinous crimes began to gradually subside. This started after the Federal Government stepped in when they began to be pressured by other states throughout the country. This pressure did not come about from these southern states. The Ku Klux Klan was a terrorist organization and it did not go away quietly into the night.

Dan, Joe's father did not participate in Ku Klux Klan activities now that he was in business. As a businessman, Dan knew some people would be offended if they knew his sympathies were still with the Ku Klux Klan, even though he kept it under necessary control. Other than Joe's juvenile behavior in his earlier years, as Joe got older, Dan did not allow him to get seriously involved with the Klan.

Dan would hunt and fish with Joe and take him on trips that were part of his business. The trips consisted of purchasing new equipment for the farm, vegetable seeds for the vegetable garden and items for keeping up his house such as paint, carpentry tools, and shrubbery which was Dan and Joe's job along with other workers on the farm. Dan was so proud to own his great big house, that he kept the outside beautiful and his wife kept the inside beautiful always buying nice expensive things and paying for expensive decorating.

During Joe's teenage years he was against those supporting the Civil Rights Movement that started under Dr. Martin Luther King Jr. Joe's sympathies were with his father and the segregationists. Joe was now on his way to college and at this time, the Civil Rights Movement was behind some of the plans to begin the integration of the elementary schools and large colleges. Joe and his father were very much against integrating the schools. It just so happened that the school Joe was going to attend was a small business college and integration had not yet reached the smaller colleges. However, Joe went to other schools shouting at people who were trying to get into these larger colleges to integrate them. When he finally got into college, he went over to visit the college where his friend Eugene was now attending as a pre-medical student. Eugene had been one of the participants with Joe against the African Americans all the way through their early school years and high school, holding the same sentiments as Joe even though he came from one of richest families in Joe's area.

In the story (The Family Secret), Joe's friend Eugene had been in private school with Joe since kindergarten. Because Eugene was from one of the wealthiest families that lived near Joe's neighborhood, Eugene was trained in his home in all the protocol that a wealthy family should follow. Joe tried to learn how the rich people lived from Eugene's example and followed his mannerisms such as how a gentleman should act however, Joe also followed Eugene's very bad behavior. The private school that they attended encouraged this behavior towards the African Americans by segregating and disrespecting them and by never correcting the White students.

Both boys attended private school all the way through high school and when they had the opportunity, they acted very mean to African Americans. The two boys laughed at and made fun of them especially, in their last years of high school. Joe and Eugene still called African Americans names from the school bus talked about their color, called them dumb and made fun of their clothing, how they talked and called them mean animal names.

The children who were being harassed tried to get out of the way when the bus was passing them. When Joe and Eugene who had stayed close all these years finally got to college, Joe along with Eugene began to learn to curb their racist behavior. Through the years they continued to stay close, even though Eugene was now in premedical school and would someday become a doctor. They talked about the Civil Rights Movement and neither one of them were for it at all, and then it happened, Joe met Carlee.

# 5

## Meeting Carlee

When Joe started his third year of college, Eugene was in his first year of medical school, because he had attended an accelerated premedical college. Joe went to see Eugene to tell him about this girl he met by the name of Carlee. He told Eugene that she was from the North and lived with her grandparents there and that her father was a practicing physician here in the South. He also told Eugene that Carlee's mother had passed away when she was only two. Joe told Eugene that he made a racist remark around Carlee and she almost had a fit. First, she let Joe know that her grandparents were from the South and that her grandfather was the head of a large pharmaceutical company in the North. When she heard Joe make that racist slur, Carlee told him right off the bat that her grandparents would never allow a racist slur like that in their house and asked Joe if he had those racist beliefs that some Southerners still did. Of course, Joe denied it and begged her pardon and he was glad to find out that not only was Carlee pretty, but a lady.

Carlee told Joe that she was majoring in science and minoring in history at her school and that her father remarried awhile after her mother died, and later on had two more children. Joe and Carlee had been dating for about three weeks and even though she came from the North, she acted just like a Southern bell except for her Northern accent.

Carlee told Joe she had a number of relatives in the area and when she told Joe who they were, he realized this girl's family was one of the richest families in the region. Joe really fell for this Carlee and knew she is the marrying type. He believed she was also a virgin but did not want to ask Carlee if she was until he got to know her better. In time though, Joe would want to know if he were to marry her. Joe realized he could not let Carlee know about his racist past, because she would hardly believe it. Carlee was pretty as a picture with very light brown hair, beautiful blue eyes, and very fair skin. She was a couple of years younger than Joe and loved the school she attended, which her grandmother and mother had also attended many years ago. The school was one of the best woman's colleges in the state.

Carlee was very articulate and the usual student slang did not come out of her mouth. Eugene stopped Joe and asked how he was going to win this girl as rough and crude as he had been? Joe did not know how, but he knew he must be a gentleman around her, because he was so in love with Carlee. Eugene then asked Joe to bring Carlee to his school so that he could meet her. Eugene felt that Joe was describing a very lovely woman and he was very anxious to meet her. When Eugene meant Carlee, he let Joe know that he had to treat this relationship with extra care. Eugene found Carlee to be an outstanding woman and as such, he let Joe know, if he did marry Carlee, he must do the right thing by her and Joe agreed.

After Joe graduated from college, he took Carlee home to meet his parents who were very pleased to meet her. After they learned who Carlee's family members were, they knew that their son Joe was moving up in the world and he was in that class of friends they always wanted him to know and be a part of. Carlee was very lovely to Joe's family and she got along with them very well. She realized Joe's father was a little crude but so nice to her that it did not bother her at all. Carlee loved how beautiful Dan and Maureen's house was, inside and out. They also had horses so Carlee and Joe could go riding together whenever she came to visit. Carlee also met several cousins of Joes who were visiting with Joe's parents. Joe was truly in love with Carlee and made every effort to keep the prejudice side of him and his family away from her. He reminded his family that Carlee was from the North and saw race relations differently than they did.

So, he asked them not to use any racial slurs in Carlee's presence. They all agreed because they knew how much Joe cared for her and they also knew what was going on in the South with the Civil Rights Movement at that time.

Carlee took Joe to meet her father, Dr. Hugh Grant, who did not live too far from where she was attending college. Dr. Grant and Joe seemed to hit it off well and even went out on a fishing trip together. Dr. Grant took Carlee's 13-year-old half-brother Michael, along with Joe and they had a really good time especially when Michael caught a medium-size fish, it was the highlight of the day. Carlee stayed home with her stepmother Kim, and her half-sister June. Together they had cooked dinner for the men when they came home from fishing. When Hugh, Joe, and Michael arrived home while having dinner, Hugh talked to Carlee about her courses at college. He was happy to know that she was considering expanding her science career toward becoming a doctor and was taking more science courses. The graduate school that Carlee planned to attend after graduating had a science program that offered sciences courses that could be applied in medical school or a graduate school that had other science programs.

Kim worked part-time because they could afford a nanny for their two children and she did not want to lose the skills she had acquired working in a top investment company. The investments that she and Hugh made together served them very well and they were on their way to becoming financially secure. To add to their financial security, Hugh's specialty was neurosurgery, so he was doing very well all by himself. Whenever Carlee visited her father, he always gave her a nice amount of money for the extra things she wanted to do at college. Carlee was blessed because both sides of her family faithfully attended church and were very sincere about their belief in God. During times when Carlee invited Joe to family dinners after church services, everyone talked about the Lord and even Joe could bring some comments into the conversation because his mother Maureen made the whole family go to church. The church Joe attended was segregated but so were most of the churches at that time in the South.

Joe, like his father, liked making money and he didn't mind working as hard as he could to make it, so even before he got married, he had accumulated quite a bit of wealth. Although he had to admit that even though Carlee came from a very well to do family, she never really seemed that interested in those things that wealthy people wanted to accumulate for themselves. Like her grandfather, Carlee was very laid back and seemed to take things in stride but always worked hard to succeed in what was important to her and her loved ones. She was an exceptional young woman.

Joe was never interested in advanced degrees but wanted to get right into the business world when he graduated. Graduation day for him finally came, Carlee still had a way to go in college but they still stayed very much interested in each other and truly enjoyed being together. Of course, this meant that Joe had to sever his ties to his bigoted lifestyle which had made him feel so confident and important and he had to admit to himself that sometimes he missed it, but Carlee was worth it. Since Carlee would go back home for spring and winter vacations, Joe worked hard during those times so that he would be ready for marriage after she graduated. He shared the knowledge of some of his investments in land and property with her and she praised him and let him know that she was very proud of him. Carlee was really pleased with academic success, maintaining high averages in college along with the many awards she won. Joe cared for Carlee so much he tried to encourage her when she had to attend an award ceremony and would go with her even though he was not one bit interested. She and Joe both liked Elvis Presley and other country singers, so whenever they could go to one of these concerts whether they were local or in other cities they tried to make them. Carlee made a friend at school named Jean who shared most of Carlee's outlook on life and soon they became best friends. She was from the South but she didn't have a lot of the racist ideas that so many of the other students had. Jean and Carlee could just be themselves with each other and it gave them relief from listening to the same points of view held by so many of the students. Carlee and Jean applied to be roommates in their last years at school and sometimes Jean would go with Carlee to her grandparent's house during vacation time. They kept their friendship even after graduation and up until Carlee married, they attended events together that they both enjoyed. They consisted of concerts, science fairs, lectures, plays and good movies. Knowing that Carlee didn't have any racist ideas encouraged Joe to keep himself in check about the attitude he had against African American people. He knew that the ideas she had from living in the North could not easily be set aside. His friend Eugene could not believe that Joe had met such a sweet girl with all the characteristics that any man would want in a wife and how bright she was which was an outstanding quality. Many Southerners who go North do change their thinking about race and are thought of as betraying their Southern brothers with their new ideologies. It was observed that most girls that had come to school from the North to the Southern colleges seemed more forward in their behavior than the Southern girls. This was not detected in Carlee at all and Eugene admitted to Joe that she was the type of woman that he would like to marry.

Carlee liked Eugene and from time-to-time Joe and Carlee double dated with Eugene and his date. Because Eugene was a medical school student, he seemed to be more intelligent than some of Joe's other friends Carlee had met and she was glad that Joe had Eugene as a friend in his life. Of course, she had no idea about the past that Joe and Eugene shared and Joe wanted it to remain that way. Courting Carlee helped Joe to become more polished and even Carlee noticed a radical change in him as the years went by. She promised to marry Joe as soon as she graduated. Carlee excelled academically like her mother Clare and her grandparents were flying South often when she received various academic awards. Many of these awards were in science and her grades stayed high.

Carlee's grandparents missed her at home especially since they had lost her mother Clare and Carlee had so many of her mother's qualities. Her grandparents supported her with whatever she needed at school and she was known to be a person that helped those who were struggling financially, with her grandparent's permission.

In her last year of college her grandfather bought Carlee her own horse named Star because of the star shape on her forehead and paid for it to be stabled close to the school. Carlee was able to visit Star and ride during the week and learned to care for her. Star was such a beautiful horse Carlee received many offers from the clients of the stable personnel to buy her but even after she graduated and she and Joe married, Carlee kept Star. Since Joe was two years ahead of Carlee, when he graduated, he put all his energy into preparing himself in business with his father's help and like his father he became very successful. By the time Carlee graduated, Joe was in the financial position not only to marry her but he could also offer her the financial security that she was used to. Though Joe lived a restrained life from what he used to do, he felt it was worth it because he loved Carlee so much and was always happy to be with her. Joe even went to church with Carlee but never heard sermons about racist hatred and what to do about it. The messages were like the same ones he received from his own church when he was growing up, so he felt his thinking was a part of the proper way he should believe and live. Now he fully realized that if he married Carlee there were some restrictions that he had to adhere to. Eugene had dropped a lot of the racist ideas he practiced in high school and by the time he was in medical school he realized that whatever color a person was, they still had the same internal and external physiology and that any race, if they had the same blood type, could give blood to another race. So, Eugene tempered his racist feelings because of his medical knowledge. He didn't verbally express this but instead avoided the subject as much as he could and steered clear of identifying himself with it. Many of students from northern states were coming to medical schools in the south and sometimes arguments about racial injustice would come up and these students would hold their own during such arguments. These Northern students made some of their Southern colleagues feel as if they were ignorant. Since the students from the North were usually from very fine undergraduate schools so, it was hard to win arguments against them. However, knowing they had come to the South from the North these Northern students tried not to let these arguments get out of hand and generally they got along very well with the Southern students.

One of the students was a Quaker from Pennsylvania. Sometimes in these heated discussions she held her own. This was because her Quaker religion had shielded African Americans for many generations. The Quakers had been persecuted for helping these people escape slavery from the 1600's through the 1800's. The Southern students realized her Quaker religion was the reason for her ideology and because of her excellent academic record, they made excuses for her rather than admit they were not right in their prejudicial thinking. Another excuse that the Southern medical students used to support their racist positions was that there were many Northerners and Westerners that were also racist. They could prove this from historical facts and usually this could not be challenged because it was true. This could be seen in some of the Civil Rights marches that took place in Northern and Western towns and surrounding communities. Like Southerners, they held the same racist feelings against African Americans. The marches in these Northern and Western towns revealed vicious attacks on the part of White people in their communities including rock throwing, physical attacks and awful name calling.

Courting Carlee helped Joe to feel better about himself and even his family noticed that he was maturing into a very fine man. Carlee feelings for Joe were growing deeper and she really wanted to marry him. She saw this change in him as she approached her last months in school and as she looked forward to their wedding.

Joe's love for Carlee was growing stronger and he made every effort to keep that prejudice side of him from her. As mentioned, he casually explained to his family again that Carlee was from the North and saw race relations differently than they did. So, Joe again, reminded his family not to use any racial slurs in Carlee's presence and they all agreed especially knowing what was going on in the south with the Civil Rights Movement at that time.

Finally, Carlee graduated and her grandparents planned a large wedding for her and Joe. Many of Carlee's cousins came from the south along with her father Hugh, stepmother Kim, half-brother Michael and half-sister June. Carlee's Aunt MaryAnn, her husband and three children, college friends, and her grandfather's friends from his company were some of the wedding guests. Carlee's grandmother requested that Carlee wear her mother's wedding gown. Her grandmother was very happy because she had done everything, she could to preserve her daughter Clare's wedding gown. The wedding was beautiful and Joe's family was very impressed with Carlee's family. So, Carlee and Joe went back South after a two-week honeymoon in Europe and Carlee started graduate school. She loved science so much she started thinking more about pursuing a career as a doctor. Joe was working hard making money which he loved and he now was paying Carlee's tuition fees and taking care of whatever was necessary for her. He loved what he was doing for Carlee because it was how his father Dan took care of his mother Maureen. She and Joe were very happy and he still remembered to keep his behavior in check. Finally, after two years, she got pregnant and they both were delighted going so far as decorating their lovely apartment and having the nursery readied for their new addition.

Carlee was studying hard and she and Joe had already decided to name the baby Clare after her deceased mother if it was a girl and Joe Jr., if it was a boy. Jean, her friend from college gave Carlee a beautiful baby shower and invited former classmates, family, and friends and there was nothing that was lacking as far as baby gifts. Carlee's father and stepmother opened a bank account for the baby in the amount of $1000.00 and bought Carlee a rocker for the nursery because she planned to nurse the baby.

Joe's mother Maureen was so pleased that Carlee allowed her to be involved with welcoming the new baby that she went all out and even purchased a pedigree poodle, which she kept at her home for when the baby grew older. Dan could not wait for the baby to come and sent Carlee a huge bouquet of flowers when she finally went into the hospital. Then something happened that nobody could explain.

Carlee delivered a baby girl with blonde hair and blue eyes that everyone at the hospital nursery was talking about. She was 8 pounds and her mother and father thought she was absolutely beautiful and Carlee's grandparents felt the same way. However, after Carlee came home from the hospital, she noticed that Joe had a serious change of behavior which she discussed with her aunt MaryAnn.

Finally, Joe admitted to Carlee what was bothering him. It was something that he overheard while standing outside the nursery, he could not be seen by anyone, however, he overheard a nurse mention to another nurse that the beautiful blonde baby in the nursery had African American blood. The nurse said she knew because of the small marking on the lower part of her back which could have been thought of as a birthmark. The nurse also mentioned that no one would have ever suspected the baby's ethnicity by looking at her. Carlee discussed this with her aunt again and began the divorce proceedings Joe requested hoping he would change his mind. As the months went on, however, Joe became more distant with Carlee and the baby and she realized she had to go back to live with her grandparents where she was wanted and loved. As Carlee promised Joe, she did not let her grandparents know the real reason for the divorce, with the agreement that he would not mention the reason to his parents and his family members. Carlee suffered depression during her time back home with the baby and was eventually placed under a psychiatrist care. The doctor was a friend of her grandfather and he took her case very seriously.

Carlee's grandparents were so glad to have her and the baby back home, they never pressured her about the reason she divorced Joe. Instead, they helped her enroll in school and go on with her life. Fortunately, by this time in Carlee's Grandparent's lives, they were financially secure. So, along with Joe's financial assistance, all but Carlee's emotional needs were met.

# 6

## Joe's Move Back Home

Joe settled back into his parent's house and gave up he and Carlee's apartment. Now that all of the younger children who had had lived off and on with Joe's parents were older, they no longer came to stay at the house except on special occasions. Because of this, Joe was home alone with his parents and was always working on ideas to improve his business with his mother's help. Dan and Maureen worried about Joe because he was still so young and they were very unhappy that he and Carlee had broken up.

They tried to find out why Joe and Carlee divorced but Joe never said anything negative about Carlee and when he did mention her it was always with kind and sweet words. Joe missed Carlee terribly, but not the baby. For some reason, even though Clare was beautiful and blonde with blue eyes like his, Joe couldn't get over the fact Clare had African American blood in her and therefore he could not have it known that this existed within his child. Although his friend Eugene had told him that the African

American blood that existed in Clare wouldn't show up, he knew that Joe would never except the child. He decided not to try to influence Joe to continue his marriage with Carlee because he wanted their friendship to remain even though he realized how deep Joe's racist feelings were.

Joe went on with his life, however, he did go back to some of his old ways that Dan had instilled in him against African Americans, including feeling superior to them. His grandfather and his great-grandfather held on to the same negative beliefs against African Americans that the Klan held. They were still laughing about their past sins in conversations to which Joe tried not to encourage. In conversations when his dad would bring up old tales about what they did to African Americans in the old days, Joe distanced himself. Doing this brought to his mind how Carlee never wanted to hear this racist talk. Joe and Eugene stayed good friends, but Eugene was very upset about Joe letting Carlee go especially since she did not know how this happened and Eugene knowing that his advice was correct. But Joe was so steeped in his attitude against African American people, that Eugene knew he could not change his mind, even though Carlee was about the best woman a man could find as a wife. Because he and Joe had been such good friends for so many years, Eugene could not let that friendship go because they genuinely cared for each other even though Eugene learned as he matured that a lot of what they had been taught as children was wrong. Also, when he traveled to these medical conferences in the North he met and saw so many African American doctors who held such prestigious positions he had to change his mind or label himself as ignorant.

When they got together, he let Joe know how he felt and told him he was sure he would regret his decision. Eugene also felt guilty because he knew he felt just like Joe until his training in medical college opened his eyes to a lot of things about race and people in general. He also could see how people who thought they were in the right about a thing can be very wrong.

Eugene was so careful about picking the right wife especially after meeting Carlee and being around her for the years she and Joe were together. Eugene wanted someone just like her and it took him quite a while to find the right woman which he eventually did. By this time in his life, he made some serious changes and as the years went on, it seemed that he and Joe both came to a better place in their thinking concerning race relations, but it took Joe much longer. He also brought Eugene up to date about all that had happened in the family which included Dan's change in his attitude towards African Americans before he passed away. Eugene could hardly believe what he had heard about the change in Joe's father Dan.

# 7

## Meeting Martha

After being away from Carlee for quite a while, Maureen suggested that Joe meet a lovely girl in their church, who like Carlee, didn't like a lot of racist conversation. This piqued Joe's interest and he told his mother he would come to church with her that Sunday to meet her. Maureen explained that she was not a beauty like Carlee but attractive enough and very proper. Maureen said that she liked her very much and that she was very active with the young people at church and stressed good character to them. Her name was Martha and she was around Joe's age. After his mother's description of her, Joe remembered to really be on his best behavior like he was with Carlee but realized even within himself that he was not ready to give up all his ideas about race. When Sunday came, he dressed very nicely and felt a little strange because he didn't think he could care for anyone like he cared for Carlee but he said to himself he would see.

After he met Martha at church, there was something about her that really attracted him to her. She seemed to have some of the same qualities that Carlee possessed. Even though Martha was attractive, she was not as beautiful as Carlee, but very feminine. When they began dating, Joe seemed to feel very relaxed when they were together. As a Christian, Joe knew Martha didn't appreciate anything coarse or crude. So, like it was with Carlee, Joe was on his best behavior.

She had a very good job and had an associate degree in business. She also had a one-year degree from Bible College in "Introduction to the Old and New Testaments", which was paid for by her church.

Martha's father farmed for a living and as the years went on and more children came, he did well enough so that she and her brother and sister did not grow up in poverty. When the children were older, her mother got a good job in a restaurant as a hostess and was able to contribute to the household income. Their house was very nice but not large like Joe's parent's house.

Martha, like Carlee, did not want to hear any kind of derogatory race talk, so Dan behaved himself. Martha got along well with Maureen and as the relationship grew, they did a lot of things together and found they had a lot in common. She became the daughter Maureen always wanted.

Martha noticed that Joe's mother did not talk much about Carlee except to say that her relatives, who they both knew as town's people were well-to-do but never mixed with Maureen and her husband. Martha planned to go back to school for a Bachelors' degree in business so that she could one day open her own business and this was a strong desire of hers. Martha worked at City Hall so she knew a lot about the community. This was good to know because of Joe and his father's businesses. She had no idea how wealthy Joe was and he wanted to keep it that way until he was sure that she was the right one for him. Except for the legal papers, Joe did not hear from Carlee even to know how their little girl Clare was doing. He always remembered how beautiful she was at 8 lbs. and how much her mother loved her.

He realized that Carlee felt he did not want any attachment to the baby so that was probably the reason she didn't send any information to him about her. Carlee heard from some of her relatives, after she and Joe were apart for more than a year, that he went back to live with his parents but since they divorced, he didn't seem to be involved in the community that much except for the involvement regarding his business. No one could get a word out of him about why he got his divorce from Carlee.

He really felt good about meeting Martha and he thought of marrying her, since similar to Carlee, she had those qualities that he really admired and had gotten used to married life. She seemed to represent how a real Christian woman should act. After going together one more year, they got married at his mother's house and of course, Maureen was so happy putting the wedding together with Martha in

Maureen's beautiful home. Martha let her have free reign, as long as she shared her ideas with her and usually everything Joe's mother suggested, Martha agreed with it.

Joe did not talk much about Carlee but he never spoke negatively about her. He never mentioned anything to Martha about the baby and didn't know if his parents had. He told Eugene about Martha telling him that he finally met someone he liked and he was glad that she had a lot in common with what he had with Carlee. His dad liked the idea that she knew a lot about farming and she did since she and her brother and sister had helped their father out when they were on their farm growing up. Joe could feel relaxed and comfortable around Martha but he had to watch his mouth and his racist behavior. He also continued to work very hard in his business.

Eugene met a wonderful woman named Sheila and married her but they didn't have children right away. His wife Shelia got along very well with Martha and Maureen and they all stayed very close together through the years. On one occasion when Eugene had to attend a doctor's conference in the area where Carlee lived, he looked her up through her medical credentials. She received her credentials after attending medical college while living with her grandparents and later on with her new husband Walter, who happened to be African American, and his parents. Eugene saw Carlee again and her new husband Walter and Joe's daughter Clare. He also saw Carlee's grandparents again. Carlee was very happy to see Eugene and was happy to know he had gotten married. When they got together, Eugene shared some of his concerns with Carlee and her husband as they were bringing each other up to date about what had happened since he last saw Carlee. Eugene was a little concerned because he and Shelia didn't have any children but they didn't want to adopt, so they were waiting patiently to conceive on their own.

Carlee was amazed when he told her this because she was now an obstetrician. She told him that she had just delivered a baby boy a week earlier and he was a very handsome little boy. The baby's parents were killed in an automobile accident and so far, the baby seemed to be fine but they were keeping him in the hospital for observation for several more days. The parents were Norwegian and it seemed their next of kin could not come to America because they were older and did not have the means to make the trip. Because the baby was still under the hospital's care, the hospital had say-so as to whom he should be given to but in a few more days, the State would come in and take over. The parents had been studying at one of the universities close to the hospital and they were originally from Norway. Carlee told Eugene that she could take him to the hospital if he would like to see the baby. Eugene always wanted a boy, so hearing all of this about the baby piqued his interest. Carlee called the hospital so they would know they were coming and they went to the newborn nursery and just as Carlee said he was a lovely baby with light brown hair. Eugene had light brown hair as well. As soon as Eugene saw him, he fell in love with him and called Shelia right away and she seemed very pleased with the news. The hospital where the baby was staying had all the proper paperwork for allowing this child to be adopted by Eugene and Shelia. What was in Eugene's favor was that Carlee was a doctor who frequently had deliveries at this hospital and also Eugene was a practicing physician and the hospital administrators who were taking care of the adoption checked out his credentials at the hospital where he worked.

Shelia flew up the next day and stayed with Walter and Carlee and went to the hospital to see the baby. Like Eugene, she fell in love with the little guy and couldn't wait to take him home. Also, she invited Walter and Carlee to visit them in the South as soon as they could. This pleased Carlee because she truly cared for Eugene as a good friend before she had married Joe and the two years afterward. She was now happy to know that she would also be a friend again to him and to his dear wife. The two couples were very excited about the baby and felt it was a true miracle.

Eugene and Shelia said they wanted to name the baby Neil, which means champion and so he went to his new home with the name Neil. They also asked Carlee and Walter, knowing that they were two Christians, if they would be their child's Godparents and they excitedly agreed.

On the way home on the plane, Eugene told Shelia that he had never been a very religious man but he truly felt in his heart that God definitely had something to do with this and that he would raise this child and any others that came along in the Christian faith. Shelia who had been hoping Eugene would become more interested in church and Christianity had been secretly praying for this change in him and now this new baby had caused this to happen. When Eugene and his wife Sheila got home with the baby, his family was so happy for both of them that his sister planned a big baby shower inviting friends and family. It wasn't long before Eugene and his wife gave up their lovely apartment and bought a home with the white picket fence and all the other typical things for children. There was even a tire in the back yard tied to the branch of one of the large trees that the former owner's children used to swing on.

When Joe heard the news, he was elated because he knew how much Eugene wanted a baby. When Eugene told him, what happened with Carlee and Walter, he felt it was a miracle as well, this seemed to increase his faith in believing in Christ even more. He felt a little bad that Eugene didn't ask him and Martha to be the godparents but he realized he did not show much interest in Christianity to Eugene. When Eugene did find out about his change in attitude, he promised that if there was another baby, Joe and Martha would be chosen as the godparents. Joe finally made up his mind to marry Martha and he did give her a beautiful engagement ring while they continued to wait to set their wedding date.

# 8

# The Wedding

Several months before their wedding, Joe said he had a wedding gift for Martha. She could pick out a house that she would like to have in the neighborhood that they would both like to live in and that he could afford. He quoted the price range that he could afford and the type of neighborhood he would also like to live in. She was so shocked that when they started visiting real estate agents, Martha felt like her dreams were coming true. It took them about a month to find a house in the neighborhood they both really liked. Joe told her that she could pick out living room and bedroom furniture and at least a table and chairs for a kitchen set to have a place to eat. He wanted furnishings before they moved in because after the wedding and before their honeymoon, he wanted to carry her over the threshold of their new home. He then planned that the next morning they would start out on their honeymoon. He thought they both would love Aruba where they would stay for two weeks. His mother would take care of his business which she had already been helping him with since he moved back in with her and his father Dan. His business was in line with his father's business, handling everything anyone would need for horticulture and his mother did a very good job with him in the business, bringing in that woman's touch by making the store very attractive.

Finally, Joe and Martha's wedding came together at Joe's mother's home. People in the community who had looked down on Maureen and her family heard from those who attended the wedding that they had never in their lives been to such a fabulous wedding. It was so beautifully put together; flowers were everywhere and the food was excellent. There were small pieces of cut cake that matched a beautiful wedding cake and surrounded it. Menus were picked up by those who were the servers from the empty plates on the round tables where the guests sat. The guests circled their choices on their menus and placed the menus back on their plates for the waiters to collect and read. The menus were marked with a table number and a ten-chair placement number at each seat around the table. They included three types of vegetables, a salad, three kinds of meat and shrimp, deep fried potatoes and fresh fruit was served in small crystal bowls placed at the top of the fork setting. There were beautiful large linen napkins that were the same color as the round linen tablecloths with beautiful stainless-steel silverware. The beautiful wedding china that was rented was so impressive that Joe's mother started getting invited to more homes of their very wealthy neighbors after the wedding was described to them.

Joe was really very happy with his new wife Martha and he was glad that he married her. Unlike Carlee, Martha was a Southerner and was more familiar with Southern ways. Their home was very peaceful except when Joe occasionally had a temper tantrum. Because of her calm and sweet disposition, Martha was able to calm him down to the point that he could not even recognize himself.

One day Joe had a situation involving an African American customer at the store. He came home complaining about how this young black man got on his nerves because his questions kept him from waiting his White customers. The man spoke very loudly and said, "If I was White like them, we would still be talking".

Joe did not answer him and continued helping those waiting for him. The customer walked out of the store even though Joe thought he was being nice and patient with him. Because of this inbred behavior, he actually believed that he was doing the guy a favor by being as patient with him as he was while holding up his White customers as the young black man continued talking. Joe did not realize that this man was from one of the African American colleges and was a professor of biology heading the department that had everything to do with plant life with the emphasis on the area of developing different species of the same plant. It was some of the other people waiting that let Joe know this and mentioned that this man was an expert in this field even though he was African American, many farmers who grew flowers called on him with outstanding results. Joe may have missed a great opportunity in getting to know this man and being an opportunist like his father he certainly mulled it over.

When Joe got home and thought about it more, he explained the situation to Martha calling the man racist language when he referred to him. He did not try to correct himself because he was so angry. After calming him down, his wife explained to him why she was against using that name to identify African Americans. She explained that when she was very young, her mother was very ill and after several days, she could no longer take care of the family. The farm kept her father very busy from morning to night and both of their families were in another county. The doctor was called and said she had pneumonia and had it too long which had weakened her. Because of Martha's parent's financial situation, they could not hire anyone to come in and take care of her chores as she continued to get worse.

A plantation owner next door to them had heard about her illness and stopped by to see Martha's father who was working out in the fields. When her husband explained to this man his situation, the man told him that one of his women workers was the one that everyone looked to when any of the hired workers were sick on his plantation and that she could get his wife back on her feet in no time. He told Martha's father that he would send her to their home to care for his wife and children until his wife was well and he would continue paying the hired worker himself as if she were still working at his place. He knew how hard Martha's father worked on his farm and he wanted to be a help. One thing he asked of her father and his wife was to treat this woman well because she was the sweetest woman he had ever met. Her name was Minnie and she was African American.

Minnie told her employer the story that when she was young, she had scarlet fever and almost died. Her parents were poor and all they could do was pray for her every day. She woke up one morning and she was well and she heard God's voice saying to her that the same way he had healed her, he would heal others through her care of them and her prayers. So even as a young girl she began this ministry. He said again to Martha's father "please do not mistreat her", because he knew she would only do them well. After explaining to his wife that Minnie was coming and what he was asked to do, Martha's mother was so grateful because she knew her strength was gone. Minnie came in the morning and when Martha's father came home the house was clean, the children were clean, breakfast, lunch, and supper had been prepared and his wife was sitting up in the bed with clean sheets, pillows and smiling. Minnie stayed several weeks. Flowers were all over the house and lovely meals were prepared for the adults and the children. Clean clothes were laid out each day and the children did little chores to help Minnie. The children were still too young to help their father on the farm as they did later. Minnie taught the children what they could do to help and she chopped wood for cool nights because of the pneumonia. Minnie told lovely Bible stories to the children and they looked forward to them in the evening. Whatever vegetables were ready for harvest, she canned so there would be extra food in the house.

By the following weekend, Martha's mother was feeling so much better that Minnie only had to come in three more days in the following week. Minnie asked Martha's mother for permission to continue praying with her each day and she agreed and was happy to receive those prayers. She certainly felt so much better since Minnie had come. Her husband, who was a racist and talked badly about African Americans was so overcome with Minnie's kindness to his wife that when she left, he gave her a lot of vegetables and fruits from his garden for canning. He also told his wife that Minnie was so kind and sweet that he would no longer call African Americans the names that he had called them since he was a little boy. Of course, his wife was so glad to hear what he said that she also made up her mind that she and her children would not treat these people the way they had in the past, even though some of her friends couldn't understand that. When Joe heard this story, even he softened his attitude and promised Martha that he wouldn't bring his racist attitude into their house in front of the children. Martha let him know how thankful she was to hear that and told him how much she loved and appreciated him. Even though

Martha didn't speak many words of affection she was very loving to him and he never doubted her love for him so, hearing her speak those words really meant a lot to him.

# 9

# The Business

After Martha's Wedding, Maureen and Martha set up an advisory booth at Joe's business. People could go there and get advice on different types of weddings. There were advisors who would handle the whole wedding, from the lowest cost weddings to the high-end weddings, if consulted, for a certain fee. It depended on what type of wedding was being planned. This gave Maureen and Martha greater prestige in the community and brought greater favor on Joe's horticultural business. In a year's time after the wedding, they had made an extra $100,000.00 in profit after expenses and it seemed that people outside their community were coming to consult about their wedding plans at Joe's business. Maureen and Martha even opened a bridal gown shop which was set up in the community. It made a way for the gowns and other wedding paraphernalia to be combined with their horticulture business. This really expanded their business due to the request for flowers which increased significantly. After that wedding, even Joe felt that his whole family had moved up in the world and he was very happy about it. Joe and Martha's life progressed well. They had three children and Martha and Maureen took over the wedding part of Joe's business with great success even expanding it to other counties. One interesting thing that happened to the business which was unusual and could not have happened unless as the years went on Joe began to make some changes for the better in his life especially toward African American people. It did not happen overnight, but as the wedding section of the business grew, one of the White workers who worked in the bridal shop had gone to an African American wedding and told Maureen and Martha that the dresses and tuxedoes in that wedding were the best she had ever seen. This was very unusual because this employee had been working for Martha and Maureen quite a long time and had seen clothing from some very expensive weddings. After inquiring about where they were purchased, she found out that a woman who was African American worked as a seamstress altering wedding attire in her home. She was married to a Mexican man who worked as a mechanic in town and was known to be the best. The seamstress met him in the Army and they got married but they had to come home to the South because both of her parents were elderly and needed help. After they had been in the home for a year her husband decided to take her to Mexico to meet his folks and they were so glad to see them. By marrying her, his family realized that it gave him the opportunity to come to the states and because he was so good in his occupation as a mechanic the town's people were happy to have him as a part of their community. They could see why he married her because she was a very pretty African American woman. Because she was a seamstress, she visited one of the shops in Mexico near her husband's home where they made dresses and tuxedoes for weddings. Because she was so talented making clothes for weddings and other occasions, she recognized the excellent quality in all of the garments that she looked at and thought about importing the outfits back home. She also knew that if they didn't have all the sizes that she could alter the clothing to fit any size that needed adjustments which was one of the specialties of her trade. Before she left Mexico, she discussed with her husband about going into business with this Mexican shop and importing many of these outfits to where they lived in the South. After explaining it to him and getting his permission, he thought it was a wonderful idea and they purchased many of these outfits to take home with them and then set out to find a store in their neighborhood where they could set up an ordering business for the clothes they received from Mexico. They were now ordering them for the patrons they were bringing into their new store. When their patrons saw the quality of the clothing and the low prices especially the wedding clothing this brought in a great profit to their new store. The Mexican store owner was made very happy because they had never made such a profit. The Mexican store owner had sense enough to know not to spread the good news of their increased income around even to close family members. They put the extra money in the bank and it was only to be handled by those close to what was happening in their business who knew what was coming in and going out by mail. When Martha and Maureen heard about the beautiful wedding clothing including not only the gowns but also formal dresses, tiaras, flower girl dresses, boys ring bearer outfits, tuxedoes, and other wedding items. Maureen and Martha were very interested and wanted to meet this seamstress knowing that she lived in their town in the colored section. Because White people hardly ever attended an African American wedding, they were never exposed to these beautiful wedding outfits and Martha and Maureen were very anxious to see what they looked like. When they asked the young lady that worked for them to introduced them to the African American seamstress and her husband she did. When Joe found out that her husband was a top mechanic, he was very interested in meeting him. It took several weeks but the ladies worked out a way that they could combine both their businesses and use the seamstress's altering skills. The seamstress's name was Gayle and her husband's name was George. Since Gayle and George found a store to bring the outfits, it was possible for Maureen and Martha to work with Gayle to bring these outfits to their own store as well as to their wedding clients. By Maureen, Martha and Gayle bringing these outfits into their store from the Mexican store at such a reduced price, they became the wealthiest women in their neighborhoods. Gayle's skills to alter wedding clothing to any size also allowed her to bring in some of her family members to help run the business. Gayle did exceptionally well managing her store on her side of town and her husband who was a hands-on guy in carpentry was able to help her with the things she wanted to improve and change in her store. Since Gayle and her husband George had been in the Army together and had been stationed up North, neither one of them was nervous around White people, so both women's shops seemed to work very well together. Joe, who was a lover of cars from his earliest years asked George if he could recommend him to some of his White friends when he heard what a good mechanic he was. This brought more and more business to George's shop. The three women were very happy together and worked very well as a team. Their new partnership seemed to soften Joe more and more and it changed his attitude toward the races especially since he got closer to George and saw how skillful he was as a mechanic.

# 10

## A Changed Man

Joe sent his children to the best schools in the North, after learning about these schools from his ex-wife Carlee. While away at school, one of Joe's three children Beth who was the oldest, majored in English and minored in Journalism. Between the two professional disciplines, she finally became a business writer of commercials that sold business products and she became very successful. As the years went on, she did start to write fiction primarily for her own enjoyment. Her dad Joe read some of these stories and out of the blue one day he suggested that she write his story. He wanted to share how his life was completely turned around from being a Southerner who hated many African American people. He had treated them very badly especially in his youth. As time went on, he gradually changed to the man that he was now who truly learned to love his fellow man no matter what race or creed that person belonged to. Since these changes from his past would be a shock to people presently living, he felt Beth could write it much better than he because of her education as a professional writer. He was also willing to have her expose in the book the bad things he had done in his life as well as the good things that came about much later. He realized that the children he had with Martha did not fully know his past life except for bits and pieces and wouldn't understand his past unless it was told. After thinking about it, Beth told him that she would try to do it for him and she could see how happy he was because she and her father had always been very close. Beth had come home on vacation to visit her mother and father in their beautiful Southern home which he inherited from his father Dan after he passed away. His mother Maureen had passed away years earlier.

Beth realized that quite a number of her family was still living except for the much older ones. Her father's former wife and her family were also still living, leaving enough people around her to give her the information that she needed. She also started researching as her father dictated information as far back as his great grandfather's day involving the Ku Klux KIan which covered a long period of time from the middle 1800's until the present. Some of these family members were in the Ku Klux Klan during the Civil Rights Movement under Dr. Martin Luther King Jr. and other civil rights leaders. Of course, Beth knew very little about this part of her father's life, neither did her other siblings.

Joe was now in his 60's and still going very strong in his business and was still married to Beth's wonderful mother Martha, who was responsible for most of Joe's change because of her faith in God. Joe started first with information about his own father and then shared information about his grandfather and his great- grandfather, who both carried out terrible behavior against the African American Community, in the early South. Of course, by this time those family members who were much older had passed away.

Joe let Beth know his grandfather and father's businesses, had been turned into very lucrative enterprises which had grown very large by this time. One of the ideas that grew his business phenomenally was importing gorgeous tall flowerpots from foreign countries such as Greece, France, Spain, Italy, and several countries from the Middle East. Not only were they large with a three-inch circular hole carved in their bottom but they were also covered with exotic designs which identified them as foreign made and they were advertised as Porch Pots. Large circular bottom dishes came with them and matched the design on the pots. These circular dishes caught the water poured over the plants or flowers in these pots and held it for several days. These beautiful large dishes were filled when the plants were watered by hand, using a large porch watering can. The watering can matched the main color in the first pot's design and was always placed back next to the first Porch Pot when the watering was completed. This particular porch may have held four or five of these large Porch Pots with the same watering can used to water each one of them. These watering cans were filled-up by a yard hose until all the Porch Pots were fully watered. The bottom dishes were also removed for washing so they looked clean and new for years along with their matching pots which were hosed down when needed. The perennial plants and flowers grew year after year without having to be replaced until they got so large, they had to be replanted in other parts of the front yards of these mansions. The new plants that replaced them were the same colors although they were different plants and flowers that were being started in these tall Porch Pots. The new plants started in these Porch Pots were planted in the same manner as the older plants which had to be removed. These plants looked so beautiful on the porches of these large mansions that owners of these homes picked very attractive expensive plants or flowers to adorn their porches and front yards. These flowers and plants were purposely matched to the beautiful colors and patterns on these pots. These Porch Pots were advertised as imported from the foreign countries previously mentioned. Because they were so different, they became a great hit on these large porches in front of these huge homes especially to those who loved flowers and plants. Many were sold throughout the years not only in the South but were shipped to many other states in the North as well. A special fish fertilizer was developed from dried fish to be added to the soil of these pots twice a year. This made the flowers and the plants grow wide and twice as tall as their normal size in these large pots. The fish fertilizer was the key and as long as it was used, these flowers and plants flourished.

This fertilizer also added great profitability to the business. Beth also learned about how her father had treated Donald, the African American man, who came into his store years ago. He did not know that this man was a biology teacher who taught at one of the African American colleges in the area near Joe's business. One of the subjects he taught was grafting plants for the purpose of bringing many different variations of colors to plants and flowers that people loved. Unknown to Joe at the time, many in Joe's neighborhood knew about Donald's expertise in this area and about his creating new colors in exotic or common plants and flowers. These were the same flowers that were later used to match those grown in the exotic Porch Pots. Though he had been very prejudiced against Donald when he was younger, as he grew older and changed his way of thinking, he and Donald became great friends and became partners in the art of grafting and growing other unusual plants.

Some of Donald's ideas won several awards in the plant world and Joe was able to display these awards in his store. Donald's ideas did much to promote Joe's horticultural business and Donald became wealthy through the ideas that he shared with Joe. As mentioned, because of Donald's ideas, Joe's income increased significantly which enabled him to send all of his children to the finest schools in the North. He offered to send his daughter Clare from his previous marriage to Carlee's school which had an excellent science program. Clare did not need the money because her grandfather, her mother and her stepfather had saved a sufficient amount of money to cover her education all the way through the completion of a master's degree.

When Clare graduated, she acquired an administrative job in her field at a prestigious hospital. Carlee his ex-wife, let my father know that a lot of the money he had sent through the years for Clare's support was also saved toward her education and they used it for the things she needed when she was away at school including lab fees, workbooks, and other items that she needed to complete her education in the scientific field. This had made my father very happy. Clare was older than I was and she used to visit me and my younger sister and brother when school was out. Clare had a beautiful room at my father's house which my mother decorated because my mother always wanted Clare to know she was special to our family. She was very close to me because we were much closer in age than my younger sister and brother. When Clare and I got older, Clare would plan for me to meet her at her college and I would stay over during weekends and we would have so much fun. During semester and holiday breaks from our schools, Clare and I would also visit her beautiful home in the North.

Clare had a handsome stepfather named Walter and you could tell that he was very much in love with her mother Carlee. When I visited them, they were always very lovely to me treating me like I was one of the family. Sometimes my family and Carlee's family vacationed together and we always had a wonderful time with lots of fun traveling to unusual and special places that were very different. Walter's parents and Carlee's grandparents would join us from time to time and my family really hated to leave Carlee's family and come back to the South. I also remembered that my father told me he saw a lot of Carlee when she was attending her mother's college in the South. So even though the years had gone by, I received a lot of information from Maryann about Carlee and my father. Carlee was very close to her aunt and told her to help me in any way she could because my dad had given me permission to write a book about his life including both positive and negative aspects.

So, after researching and discussing a lot of things with those around my age or a little older who were still living in my father's family, I now understood what my father meant about how he was truly changed by God into a different man. I have to pause here because I know my mother had a lot to do with the change in him. Sometimes, it was very difficult for me to hear about my father's family, his early life, and the racial prejudice that they were all involved in. I found it awfully hard to learn about his early life because it was so foreign to the man that I now know. I knew some of my father's family still carried racist ideas but not to the extreme that he practiced them when he was a much younger man.

When I think of Donald, his African American friend the biologist, and how close he and dad became through the years while working with exotic plants, I have to shake my head. I can hardly believe how racist my dad was toward him when they first met in my dad's business in those early years. To help me with the book, I also read a lot about the Civil Rights Movement and my eyes were opened to a lot of negative things that happened to African Americans in the South during the early years of my father's life and just to think that his father's family was a part of it. Most of it was so hard to believe, when I see how wonderful my father is to everybody today. The book became very popular and sold many copies adding another financial windfall to my father's fortune. Since the book continued to sell over the years, he gave a lot of the proceeds to several African American colleges to help them improve their academic excellence. He put me in charge of this project since I had continued taking educational courses until I received a doctorate degree. This helped me to become an expert in improving the educational excellence of these colleges. I have to add here that at one of the colleges that I was working with, I met my husband who was an African American man who I thought was so handsome and smart that meeting him actually took my breath away. I knew that my father Joe had really changed when he and my mother Martha gave their blessing to our desire to get married.

I have to sadly say that after our marriage, we moved to the North knowing that an interracial marriage would have a better chance of surviving there. Both our doctorate degrees in education helped us to receive jobs in universities which were very lucrative. To my joy, my husband was a believer from a strong Christian family and he was responsible for introducing me to very strong Christian believers who helped me to strengthen my own faith. We had a boy and a girl which I thought as their mother were two of the world's most beautiful children and my father Joe and my mother Martha agreed.

## THE END

# About the Author

Janice Freeman was born in New York City in 1936. She is now the last person living in her immediate family. She grew up in the Bronx with two older brothers, and her parents were Ben and Mattye Watson. The family moved from New York when

Janice was 11 years old. Their move was to a lovely community in Verona, New Jersey. The three children finished Henry B. Whitehorne High School which was academically excellent and considered to be one of the finest schools in the Nation. From this school, Janice learned to read classical novels which she loved. This encouraged her to appreciate good film and artwork especially the Masters. Janice married after her second year of college. After graduating college, she went into a banking career, never thinking about writing. She later had two children, a son and a daughter. Janice earned a master's degree from Fitchburg State College, Fitchburg, Massachusetts. She also became a Pastor later in life and pastored her own church in the state of Massachusetts. Janice was in her early 70s when she decided to retire. She wanted to write a book at least by the age of 80 and had gained enough knowledge to help her in this endeavor. She wanted the book to show a different side of the affects of racial injustices on White life in America opposed to only seeing how African Americans were affected. This was started in her first book "The Family Secret" and finished as a sequel in this second book titled "Joe".